Quick Quips & Quotes

By

Daniel & Dorothy Josipovich

Lake Forest, Ca. 92630

A collection of quips, quotes and humorous sayings

Dedication

This book is dedicated to my wife Dorothy who, for forty five years, has supported my every effort. When she wasn't cooking, cleaning, babysitting and other mundane things like ironing and shopping, she typed everything I wrote.

She took an interest in the "Quips" and worked with me to assemble them. Her comments like, "Don't you dare print that", kept the book in focus.

Thank you for your tireless efforts and sense of humor.

I Love you.

Foreward

"Three minutes of excitement packed into three hours" is a quip that very well describes how we live our lives. I have found that the worth while exciting moments are usually found in a few seconds, minutes or, if you're fortunate, a few hours.

Most days of your commute to work you won't remember but when an inconsiderate driver cuts you off or takes your parking place by executing an illegal left turn in front of you the adrenaline burst causes you to remember that day.

You may not remember all the days of the pregnancy but the delivery day is a whole new event. That minute on the beach at sunset paints an indelible picture in your mind. If one could only stop that moment and make it last longer.

Someone speaks and describes in only a few words the way you feel about your spouse, the government, your in-laws and a hundred other things. That saying is then remembered and becomes your personal vignette on life.

In this booklet I have tried to capture those moments in words. Some humorous, some ponderable and others spiritual or inspirational.

Only a few of them are my own.

Quick Quips & Quotes

Hell lies not in torture.
            Hell lies in an empty heart.

The hurrier I go, the behinder I get.
            Pennsylvania Dutch saying

Integrity – when you do the right thing
            even when no one is watching.

There are three kinds of people;
            *the ones that can count
                . . .and the ones that can't.*

Life is a succession of moments.
            To live each one is to succeed.
            Corita Kent

Great works are performed not by
strength but by perseverance.

Samuel Johnson

A wagging tail is more sincere
than many handshakes.

I 've always tried to go a step past
wherever people expected me to end up.

Beverly Sills

E ven if you're on the right track,
you'll get run over if you just sit there.

Will Rogers

2

Quick Quips & Quotes

Q. *Why do they call it golf?*

A. *Because all of the other four letter words were taken.*

When you reach for the stars,
   you may not quite get them,
      but you won't come up with a
         handful of mud either.

Leo Burnett

A man can succeed
   at almost anything for which he has
      unlimited enthusiasm.

Charles M. Schwab

*T*he early worm gets the bird.

*W*omen have to summon up courage
to fulfill dormant dreams.

Alice Walker

*T*hose who act receive the prizes.

Aristotle

*B*etter ruined ten times than dead once.

Yiddish Proverb

*A*ccomplishments have no color.

Leontyne Price

Some people think they're generous
  because they give away free advice.

The early bird gets the worm.
  Personally, I'd rather have a donut.

D.J.

The most welcome person is the one
  that knows when to go.

I think success has no rules,
  but you can learn a lot from failure.

Jean Kerr

Carpenter - I've cut it twice
and it's still too short.

Well done is better than well said.

Benjamin Franklin

Husband to wife:
I was not yawning!
I was trying to say something.

Eighty percent of success is showing up.

Woody Allen

A man can make what he wants of
himself if he truly believes that he
must be ready for hard work
and many heartbreaks.

Thurgood Marshall

W hen trying to make something of
yourself be careful not to
make an ass of yourself.

D.J.

I t is better to be young in your failures
than old in your successes.

Flannery O'Connor

When you own your own business
you only have to work half a day.
You can do anything you want
with the other 12 hours.

Destiny is not a matter of chance;
it is a matter of choice.
It is not a thing to be waited for;
it is a thing to be achieved.

William Jennings Bryan

Why are there more old drunks
than old doctors?

The trouble today is that many people think that you don't need road manners if you're a ten ton truck.

Unless you try to do something beyond what you have already mastered, you will never grow.

Ronald E. Osborn

Always behave like a duck — keep calm and unruffled on the surface but paddle like the devil underneath.

Lord Barbizon

You can't build your reputation
on what you're going to do.

Henry Ford

Show me a person who has never made a
mistake and I'll show you somebody
who has never achieved much.

Joan Collins

Nothing increases your golf score
more than witnesses.

What we call results are beginnings.

Ralph Waldo Emerson

Quick Quips & Quotes

It takes twenty years to make
                    an overnight success.

Eddie Cantor

To really enjoy the fire
                    try chopping your own wood.

Behind every successful man
                    there's a lot of unsuccessful years.

Bob Brown

If you have something to hide,
                    don't let Kenneth Starr
                              hear about it.

D.J.

H eroes are made in the hour of defeat.
Success is, therefore, well described
as a series of glorious defeats.

Mohandas K. Gandhi

F eeling gratitude and not expressing it
is like wrapping a gift
and not giving it.

S uccess is never final
and failure never fatal.
It's courage that counts.

George Tilton

*R*ockefeller once explained
the secret of success.
"Get up early, work late and strike oil."

Joey Adams

*B*ehind every successful man there is a
woman....nagging and nagging.

D.J.

*Y*ou see things and you say, "Why?"
But I dream things that never were
and I say, "Why not?"

George Bernard Shaw

*L*ord, grant that I may always
desire more than I can accomplish.

Michangelo

Of course there is no formula for success except, perhaps, an unconditional acceptance of life and what it brings.

Arthur Rubinstein

OSHA – Isn't that the killer whale at Seaworld?

If you really want something, you can figure out how to make it happen.

Cher

You can't think and hit the ball at the same time.

Lawrence Peter "Yogi" Berra

Quick Quips & Quotes

Louis Armstrong – wasn't he the first man on the moon?

Success is relative; it is what we can make of the mess we have made of things.

T.S. Eliot

The dedicated life is the life worth living. You must give with your whole heart.

Annie Dillard

The only place where success comes before work is in a dictionary.

Vidal Sassoon

A partheid –
    Isn't that a building in Athens?

H uman success, like human failures,
    are composed of one action at a time
    and achieved by one person at a time.
    Patsy H. Sampson

A dvertising –
    the science of arresting the human
        intelligence long enough
        to get money from it.

T he first one gets the oyster;
        the second gets the shell.
    Andrew Carnegie

16

*B*aker to customer;
    Don't bother me now, I'm on a roll.

D.J.

*T*he difference between a successful
    person and others is
        not a lack of strength,
            not a lack of knowledge,
                but rather a lack of will.

Vince Lombardi

*W*hat if they had a war
            and nobody showed up?

*I*t's not a successful climb unless
            you enjoy the journey.

Dan Benson

*B*e not afraid of going slowly;
    be only afraid of standing still.

Chinese Proverb

*T*oday it costs more to amuse the child
    than it did to educate the parents.

*S*uccess is never a destination —
    it's a journey.

Satenig St. Marie

*J*ust keep going.
    Everybody gets better
        if they keep at it.

Ted Williams

Quick Quips & Quotes

Success covers many blunders.

George Bernard Shaw

*You can't get rid of poverty
by giving people money.*

*Put your heart, mind, intellect and soul
even to your smallest acts.
This is the secret of success.*

Sivananda Sarasvati

*I've never sought success in order to get
fame and money; it's the talent and
the passion that count in success.*

Ingrid Bergman

Not failure, but low aim, is crime.

James Russell Lowell

Be not afraid of greatness;
some are born great, some achieve
greatness, and some have greatness
thrust upon them.

William Shakespeare

Keep away from people who try to belittle
your ambitions. Small people always
do that, but the really great ones
make you feel that you too,
can become great.

Mark Twain

The worst moment for the atheist is when
he feels thankful and has
no one to thank.

As long as you're going to think anyway,
think big.

Donald Trump

Just go out there and
do what you've got to do.

Martina Navratilova

Just don't give up trying to do what you
really want to do...
Where there's love and inspiration,
I don't think you can go wrong.

Ella Fitzgerald

O ccasionally you meet a person who
thinks he is
all seven wonders of the world.

I do want to get rich but I never want to do
what there is to do to get rich.

Gertrude Stein.

T he Wright brothers flew right through the
smoke screen of impossibility.

Charles F. Kettering

N othing great was ever achieved
without enthusiasm.

Ralph Waldo Emerson

Quick Quips & Quotes

*There is no point at which you can say;
"Well, I'm successful now,
 I might as well take a nap."*

Carrie Fisher

*It is better to keep your mouth shut and
appear stupid than it is to speak
and remove all doubt.*

*You may be disappointed if you fail,
but you are doomed if you don't try.*

Beverly Sills

*Keep in mind that neither success
nor failure is ever final.*

Roger Babson

The reason worry kills more people than work does is because more people worry than work.

Becoming number one is easier than remaining number one.

Bill Bradley

Those who dare to fail miserably can achieve greatly.

Robert F. Kennedy

Sometimes it is more important to discover what one cannot do than what one can do.

Lin Yutang

Quick Quips & Quotes

Rule of survival;
pack your own parachute.

T.L. Hakala

I always turn to the sports page first.
The sports page records
people's accomplishments:
the front page nothing
but man's failures.

Supreme Court Justice Earl Warren

The road to success is always
under construction.

Arnold Palmer

When you see a political situation you
don't understand, look for the
financial interest.

I don't know the key to success,
but the key to failure
is trying to please everybody.

Bill Cosby

T here is only one success –
to be able to spend your life
in your own way.

Christopher Morley

F ools despise wisdom and instruction.

Proverbs 1:7

T he will to succeed is important, but
what's even more important is
the will to prepare.

Bobby Knight

26

Quick Quips & Quotes

*T*here isn't a person anywhere that isn't
capable of doing more
than he thinks he can.

Henry Ford

*N*ever let the fear of striking out
get in your way.

George Herman "BABE" Ruth

*S*uccess and failure are both
greatly overrated.
But failure gives you a
whole lot more to talk about.

Hildegard Knef

*S*uccess in the modern world
takes far more than knowledge.

Alice L. Dement

Do something.
Either lead, follow or
get out of the way.

Ted Turner

Act as if it were impossible to fail.

Dorothea Brande

Always bear in mind that your own
resolution to success is more
important than any other one thing.

Abraham Lincoln

What small potatoes we all are,
compared with what we might be!

Charles Dudley Warner

Quick Quips & Quotes

My hard disk crashed. I had to give my computer mouse to mouse resuscitation.

I have the Tyson-Holyfield fight on a CD. It only used 2 bytes of memory.

You have a lot to lose when you only have your asterisk.

Babies take nine months to download.

The closest one can get to perfection is on a resume'.

D iplomacy – the art of knowing
what not to say.

W hat is important in a dress
is the woman wearing it.

R emember the poor and needy...
it costs you nothing.

T o have something to do
is man's only happiness.

N ecessity is the mother of
taking chances.

Mark Twain

Necessity is a mother.

D.J.

People quarrel because
      they don't know how to argue.

Washington D.C. A place where
    politicians don't know which way is
      up and taxes don't know
         which way is down.

You're never as good as anyone tells you
    when you win..
       and never as bad as they
         say when you lose.

Columbus gets a lot of grief for
discovering America. He didn't do it
on purpose you know.

Why do boring people never get hoarse?

Life is like a twenty-mule team:
unless you're the lead mule,
the scenery is all about the same.

OK, so I'm fat but you're ugly
and I can diet.

Quick Quips & Quotes

K nowing the boss's girlfriend
is called job security.

N othing wilts faster than the laurels
you rest on.

O ld timer - someone who can remember
when bacon, eggs and sunshine
were good for you.

T he exercise that really changes your
life is walking down the aisle.

A man in love is not complete
until he's married.
Then he is finished.

M y wife had plastic surgery last week.
I cut up her credit cards.

I never eat anything whose ingredients
I can't pronounce.

W ise men talk because they have
something to say:
Fools talk because they have
to say something.

Quick Quips & Quotes

Mankind can travel much faster now
but we still don't know
where we're going.

Always assume that no one
will keep it a secret.

I'm not going to buy my kids
an encyclopedia. Let them walk
to school like I did.

Love is the only thing you can't have....
until you give it away.

*T*he tobacco industry reports that it provides jobs for 2.3 million Americans not including physicians, nurses, hospital employees, drug manufacturers, fire fighters, dry cleaners, respiratory specialists, oxygen bottlers and pharmacists as well as morticians and gravediggers.

*A*ll men make mistakes but married men hear about them a lot sooner.

*E*asy street is a blind alley.

*W*rinkles should only show where the smiles have been.

It doesn't matter if you win or lose...
until you lose.

How many people work at the Pentagon?
About half of them.

Of all the animals
man is the only one that lies.

Mark Twain

Of all the animals man is the only
one that blushes... or needs to.

Mark Twain

And they lived happily ever after
                   is a fairy tale.

D.J.

I got off at the wrong exit on the freeway.
          I had to.
     The car under mine went that way.

He who loses his head
                is the last one to miss it.

If Darwin was right,
     my dog should have learned
          to operate the can opener by now.

Quick Quips & Quotes

Driving on the freeway proves that there
are more horse's asses than horses.

There is nothing wrong with teenagers that
reasoning with them won't aggravate.

A bad situation that drifts away always
comes back worse.

Do you walk to work or carry a lunch?

Is it colder in the winter than it is
on the side of a mountain?

*W*hat this country needs is more
unemployed technicians.

A dyslexic agnostic doesn't believe in Dog.

*F*ACT
43.3% of all statistics are meaningless.

*T*he wages of sin is death...
but after taxes all you have left
is a bad feeling.

Quick Quips & Quotes

The alternative to intelligence is silence.

The difference between "tax avoidance" and "tax evasion" is 10 years.

Minds, like parachutes, work only when open.

I'm beside myself with schizophrenia.

I'm definitely, positively, maybe decisive.

I sentence you to hang by the neck
until you cheer up.

It said, "insert disk #3"
but only 2 will fit.

Why experiment on animals
with so many lawyers out there?

As I said before, I never repeat myself.

Are you illiterate? Write to us
for our free book "How to Read".

Quick Quips & Quotes

Just fill out one simple form
and win an IRS audit.

Kleenex Von Trapp playing
in the Sound of Mucous.

Thank you for not annoying
me more than you do.

Everyone is entitled to my opinion.

I don't know what apathy is
and I don't care.

*T*oday's leading cause of statistics is guns.

*Y*our home and many luxury cars have
more computing power than many
third world countries.

*D*emocracy – four wolves and a lamb
voting on lunch.

*T*hesaurus – a prehistoric lizard
with an excellent vocabulary.

*S*eriously now, would you trust
a politician to run the country?

Quick Quips & Quotes

Drunk – *operator trace this call
and tell me where the hell I am.*

Three things happen when you get old.
*First your memory goes
and ... um...um*

Hire teenagers -
while they still know everything.

Lawyers – *the larval form of politicians.*

No sense being pessimistic.
It wouldn't work anyway.

*W*hy does Teflon stick to the pan?

*H*ey! Who uncorked my lunch?

*B*etter a bug than a bug on a windshield.

*W*hy can't women put
        the toilet seat back up?

*Y*ou can't leap a chasm in two leaps.

Quick Quips & Quotes

*T*he buck doesn't even slow down here!

*D*on't confuse malice with stupidity.

*F*ine – a tax for doing wrong.
Tax – a fine for doing fine.

*I*f you think talk is cheap – hire a lawyer.

*I*t's a small world but I wouldn't
want to paint it.

Don't be a sexist. Broads hate that.

Are you making progress if
         each mistake is a new one?

When you're over the hill,
            you pick up speed.

A little knowledge isn't enough.

Of course you can trust our government!
            Just ask any Indian.

Quick Quips & Quotes

Life's not passing me by.
                    It's running me over.

At the end of the game, the king and the
            pawn go back into the same bag.

California has its' faults.

If at first you don't succeed,
                    don't try skydiving.

Multitasking – screwing up
                    everything at once.

Cheerios are donut seeds.

I am not a violent person and
　　　　if you say that again, I'll kill you.

Don't take life too seriously.
　　　　　　　It'll soon be over.

The biggest problem with political jokes
　　　　is that they get elected.

It is smart to forgive your enemies
　　　　but smarter not to forget their names.

Quick Quips & Quotes

Wife to husband – *"You have 2 choices
for dinner tonight".
"Take it or leave it"*

My mind isn't so open
that just anything can crawl in.

A conclusion happens
when you get tired of thinking.

Monopoly? No!
We just don't want competition.

Bill Gates

I have no prejudices.
I hate everyone equally.

*History is a set of lies
        agreed upon by those in charge.*

*It's true: Two can live as cheap as one
        but only for half as long.*

*War never decided who was right,
        only who was left.*

Life is sexually transmitted and terminal.

*There's one thing computers can't replace.
Good old fashioned human stupidity.*

Quick Quips & Quotes

Get a charge out of life.
Hug an electric fence.

A crowded elevator smells
different to a dwarf.

There was no good reason for it.
Just government policy.

As a young man I started out with
nothing and I still have most of it.

A penny saved is an IRS oversight.

Toes – devices for finding furniture legs in the dark.

In any organization there is always at least one person who knows what's going on, but he is always identified and fired.

Nothing is so simple that it can't be screwed up.

If you save time, where do you keep it?

Quick Quips & Quotes

I proofread this book
to make sure I didn't any words out.

B eware of strong drink. It can make you
shoot at tax collectors...and miss.

T he surest sign of wisdom
is constant cheerfulness.

Montaigne.

O nce in a while you will stumble upon the
truth but most of us manage to pick
ourselves up and hurry along
as if nothing had happened.

Winston Churchill

Dreams are real while they last.
                              So is life.

Without law and order
                    our nation cannot survive
                                        Adolph Hitler

The world moves straight ahead not like
                    an arrow, but like a boomerang.

If I am chained to the wall but not being
                    whipped, am I not still suffering?

Sometimes I feel like a 3 pound hen
trying to lay a 4 pound egg.

The ruling class has the schools and press
under its' thumb.
This enables it to sway the
emotions of the masses.

Albert Einstein.

The finest steel has to go
through the hottest fire.

I love mankind:
it's the people I can't stand.

*T*he law does not pretend to punish everything that is dishonest.
That would seriously
interfere with business.

Clarence Darrow

*T*he worst penalties are always imposed on
those seeking to help the oppressed.

*O*ur purpose is not to understand the
world, but to change it.

*L*osing one glove isn't bad
but throwing the other one away and
then finding the first one, is.

Quick Quips & Quotes

A physician can bury his mistakes but a
contractor can only suggest
that the customer plant vines.

T he more I know men,
the more I like dogs.

L et's kick their ass and
get the hell out of here.
Gen. George Armstrong Custer

A rose smells better than cabbage
but does it make a better soup?

I don't always know what I'm talking about
but I know I'm right.
Muhammad Ali

59

There is no cure for birth and death.
enjoy the interval.

We need to clean up the air
and treat the animals fair.

Today I saw a red and yellow sunset and
thought... how insignificant I am!
Of course, I thought that
yesterday too,
and it was raining.

Woody Allen

Beer does not make you fat. It makes you
lean.... against bars, poles and tables.

Quick Quips & Quotes

L ove your enemies.
It really pisses them off.

A dult books are designed
for those who are not.

C old fronts, low-pressure areas and week-ends are the primary
cause of bad weather.

D rink and the world drinks with you.
Swear off and you drink alone.

You can't get rich in politics
unless you're a crook

Harry Truman

The usual masculine disillusionment is
discovering that a woman
has a brain.

Margaret Mitchell.

Time wounds all heels.

There are days when it takes all I've got
just to keep up with the losers.

Quick Quips & Quotes

We need a law that will allow a voter to
sue a candidate for breach of promise.

There's no point in speaking
unless you can improve on the silence.

Nations die on the soft bed of luxury.

Q. Do you think the terms of congressmen
should be limited?
A. No. They should stay in jail as long
as anyone else would.

*T*here are 3 parties in Washington D.C.
Democratic, Republican and cocktail.

*T*he candidate for vice president either
gets the job and then has nothing to
do or loses the job
and goes back to work.

*L*etter to the president from an American
Indian:
"Be careful with your immigration laws.
We were careless with ours."

*T*he difference between genius and
stupidity is that genius has its limits.

*N*ever eat more than you can lift.

Miss Piggy

Quick Quips & Quotes

S ure, keep your feet on the ground
but keep them moving.

M uddy water left to stand will clear.

T he man who waits will only grow
whiskers.

Y ou can measure the progress of
civilization by who gets the applause –
the clown or the thinker.

When I was a child I was told
    that anybody could become president.
        I'm beginning to believe it.

Learning about software
        is like nailing jelly to a tree.

A man about to speak the truth
    should keep one foot in the stirrup.

You have to love life to live it
        and vice versa.

Quick Quips & Quotes

For every complicated problem
there is a simple, easy to understand,
wrong answer.

You have to decide to ride the waves
or make them.

A person can be worth a million dollars
and still be worthless.

You can be a king, a conqueror or
president but when you die,
you're a mere man.

*M*ost people like to talk; the more refined
ones can force themselves to listen.

*F*ear not that your life will someday end.
Fear only that you do nothing with it.

*P*eople don't love us for our virtues.
Those they tolerate and
sometimes resent. They love us
for our human fallibility.

*T*here is a time when we must choose our
course or the drift of events
will make the decision.

Quick Quips & Quotes

I n time, we learn to trust the future
                              for our answers.

T he value of marriage is not that adults
                produce children but that
                              children produce adults.

H eaven never helps the man
                              who will not act.

N obody who ever did his best regretted it.

T here are no office hours for champions.

othing is work unless you'd rather
be doing something else.

George Halas

ootball is not a contact sport.
Football is a collision sport.
Dancing is a contact sport.

Duffy Daugherty.

lways spread out the credit
and never point fingers.

Ken Anderson

ever get into an argument
about cesspools with an expert.

ver let yesterday take up
too much of today.

Quick Quips & Quotes

Forget the past; the future
will give you plenty to worry about.

If you're killing time, it's not murder.
It's suicide.

Once a day, do something nice
for somebody else.

Don't talk too much or too soon.

If you want to catch more fish,
use more hooks.

If you hate your job, don't worry.
You won't have it long.

There is no economy
in buying cheap equipment.
Buy only the best.

I can't believe God put us on this earth
to be ordinary.

There are a thousand reasons for failure
but not one excuse.

Motivation is simple. You eliminate those
who aren't motivated.

A real executive goes around with a
worried look on his assistants.

Vince Lombardi

L eadership is demonstrated.
Not announced.

I f you're not in the parade, you watch it.

I n life, it's always fourth-and-one.
You gotta go for it.

*T*he greatest accomplishments occur
not when you do something for
yourself but when you do
something for other people.

Ronnie Lott

*I*ndividual commitment to a group effort
is what makes a team work,
a company work,
a society work,
a civilization work.

Vince Lombardi

*T*he sun doesn't shine
on the same dog every day.

*C*oaches have to watch
for what they don't want to see
and listen for what
they don't want to hear.

John Madden

Quick Quips & Quotes

You can motivate better with kind words
than you can with a whip.

Experience is not what happens to a man.
It's what a man does
with what happens to him.

Chuck Knox

If you aren't fired with enthusiasm,
you'll be fired with enthusiasm

Vince Lombardi

Always remember that Goliath
was a 40 point favorite over David.

I never eat anything I can't pronounce.

I could have been a Rhodes scholar
                if it wasn't for my grades.

We live life forward but
                understand it only backwards.

Sometimes we learn life
        not from what we experience
                but from what we escape.

Egotism is the anesthetic that dulls
                the pain of stupidity.

76

Quick Quips & Quotes

I 've tried several occupations but decided
to quit while I was still at the bottom.

I f you get run out of town, make it look
like you're leading a parade.

D oubt everything or believe everything.
Either way will save
you from thinking.

I t takes 20 years to build a reputation and
only a few minutes to destroy it.

Cheerful people resist disease
better than grumpy ones.

Books are great! They're so easy to
rewind. Just close the book and
you're right back at the beginning.

Last year the White House complained to
Hollywood that there was
too much sex in the movies.

Billy Crystal at the Academy Awards

Transportation always caused pollution.
The difference between the early 1900's
and now is that the pollution then
helped the apples grow.

*The scientists say that life evolved from
primordial slime. Evidence of that
exists with some of our politicians.*

When you're in a hole, stop digging!

*Son to father:
I want to marry a woman who's
beautiful! I want to marry a woman
who can cook! I want to marry a
woman who will
make me happy!
Father to son: Make up your mind!*

*T*he second thing to go is the mind...
     I can't remember
                    what the first one is.

*M*y mother always told me;
     "Eat everything in your plate.
There's a lot of starving children in China."
Now that I weigh 240 pounds I really don't
know how it's helping any Chinese kid.

*C*harm works well for about 15 minutes.
     After that, you'd better know something.

*E*ven flying requires resistance.

Quick Quips & Quotes

*I found the secret to happiness
but the FDA won't let me release it.
They said it was addictive.*

*Learn from your mistakes.
That way they will seem worthwhile*

*Plans don't work unless they immediately
degenerate into hard work.*

*My tongue got stuck in my eyetooth and I
couldn't see what I was saying.*

Why are mothers happy when their sons
get married and cry when their
daughters do?

Success only happens to lucky people.
Ask any failure.

Oh well, maybe I'll be smart
when I get old.

D.J.

I feel so good today I can barely stand it.
I know I'm right because
my wife just told me that
she can't stand me either.

D.J.

82

Mexican weather forecast –
   Chili today but hot tamale.

On the road of life there are passengers
   and there are drivers.

VW Commercial

Russian weather forecast –
   tonight it will be dark.

Everyone wants to live long
   but no one wants to get old.

There are two great tragedies in life.
One is not getting what you want
and the other is getting what you want.

If politicians were paid
according to what they were worth,
not many would want the job.

It's not who you know,
it's whom you know.

Truthful words are not always beautiful;
beautiful words are
not always truthful.

A *good day is one spent in good company.*

A *pessimist is one who complains about the noise when opportunity knocks.*

I *f a man is walking in the woods and he speaks to himself, is he still wrong?*

I *f a woman is walking in the woods and she speaks to herself, is she still right?*

When I retired my wife went out
and got a job.

Why put it off until tomorrow
if you can squirm out of it today?

Policeman to Shakespeare;
Wither goest thou; to a conflagration?

Congressman to senator; "Hey, a billion
here, a billion there - pretty soon
you're talking big money."

A window of opportunity is frequently
a door to success.

Quick Quips & Quotes

People are not like dogs. I've never
owned a dog that was stupid enough
to bite me while I was feeding him.

Stressed? Your cope runneth over.

You can never be famous for what you
said until you're famous for what
you did. It also helps if you're dead.

God gives us each a pocketful of time
to use however we wish.
Just remember that you can't
get back any that you waste.

Give a man a fish and he will eat for a day. Teach him how to fish and he will sit in a boat and drink beer all day.

Getting an idea should be like sitting down on a pin. It should make you jump up and do something.

E.L. Simpson

God has answered all of my prayers. Quite often He said, "No".

Don't worry! Things will go along like this for a long time. Then, for some unexplainable reason, they'll get worse.

Quick Quips & Quotes

Politicians cannot have an enema
for fear of brain damage.

Isn't it great to have complete control
over how you pay your taxes?
Cash, check or money order.

In Maine there's a saying;
"there's no point in speaking
unless you can improve on silence."

Edmund Muskie.

Even great nations can die
on the bed of luxury.

When I think of a woman,
    I think of a man. Then I take away
       reasoning and accountability."

Jack Nicholson in the movie "As Good As It Gets."

A thousand years ago everyone knew the
world was flat. Five hundred years ago
everyone knew the world was round. Right
now everyone knows that there's no such
thing as an alien. What will we know
       tomorrow?"

Adapted from the movie "Men In Black."

More than half of all the people
    who have ever lived will be alive to
       greet the new millenium.

Quick Quips & Quotes

A new medical field has recently evolved. Psychoceramics. It was developed specifically for crackpots.

G overnment, both state and federal, has interfered so much with child rearing that it can be called a monumental screw-up.

O f course I love my country! I just don't trust our government.

E verybody is a fool in someone's opinion.

You know all those cards that fall out of a magazine and those thick pages that force it to open to that page? Well, the first thing I do is tear them out and throw them all away without reading them.

D.J.

The reluctance to put away childish things may be the secret of happiness.

D.J.

You know you're in trouble when, after explaining all of the problems with your computer to a technician, his response is "Bummer, man!"

Wouldn't you like to have a one-on-one
conversation with
Einstein or Beethoven or
Plato or Jesus?

D.J.

What we really need
on television is intelligence.

Kareem Abdul Jabar has decided to be
frozen after his death so that he can later be
cloned. His clone will be known as
the "iced Kareem clone."

The world would have fewer wars and
conflicts if schools had all the money they
needed and the armed forces had to have
bake sales to buy tanks and bombers.

A man's true worth can be measured
by the things be pursues.

O ne always has time
for the things one puts first.

W ealth lies not in the things one owns
but in the lack of wants.

Y ou never leave a place you love.
You take part of it with you and
leave a part of yourself behind.

K indness – ability to love people
more than they deserve.

Quick Quips & Quotes

Love is blind; it doesn't see many faults.

A gentle word is never lost or wasted.

D.J.

A wonderful part of our nature
is our need to love something.

A burden is never too heavy
if everyone lifts.

God wants us to be comforters,
not comfortable.

You can't change the past
but you can ruin the present
by worrying about the future.

I would rather be the man who bought the
Brooklyn Bridge than the
man who sold it.

Will Rogers.

We should love those who point out our
faults, but we don't.

No one resents kind words.

When your temper gets the best of you,
it reveals the worst of you.

Quick Quips & Quotes

Humility is not thinking little of yourself; rather it is simply not thinking of yourself.

Never do anything for which you would not have the courage to ask the blessings of heaven.

Choices are the hinges of destiny.

Dig a well from which another may draw.

We, on our side, are praying to Him to give us victory because we believe we are right; but those on the other side pray Him, too, for victory, believing that they are right. What must He think of us?

Abraham Lincoln

It is better to build strong children
             than try to repair adults.

To err is human - to moo — bovine.

It is only at the tree loaded with fruit
             that men throw apples.

Quick Quips & Quotes

You can do more than pray –
       but only after you have prayed.

Joy in your heart shows on your face.

Sometime to say nothing shows
       a good command of the language.

It takes more than a soft pillow
       to ensure sound sleep.

Prosperity is an instrument to be used –
       not worshipped.

Everyone smiles in the same language.

Destroy your enemies.
Make them your friends.

Beware of your little sins.
Mosquitoes drink more
blood than lions.

Freedom is not the right to do as you
please, but the liberty to do
as you ought.

Quick Quips & Quotes

Good leaders are judged
      not by the numbers lead,
            but the numbers served.

We can never know the love of the parent
      until we become a parent.

Swallowing your pride never tastes good
      but it does not cause indigestion
          and it will cause you to sleep better.

It is better that the truth offends you
          than to conceal it.

Man has created about
33,000,000 laws but hasn't
improved on the
Ten Commandments.

Having your eyes washed out
with tears sometimes changes
the way you see things.

It is easy to make a mountain
out of a molehill.
All you do is add dirt

I am an old man and have
known a great many troubles,
but most of them never happened.

Mark Twain.

Quick Quips & Quotes

*T une your instrument first
        then have your concert.*

*B ad officials are elected
        by good people who don't vote.*

*T he things we hold tightest we lose. The
    only things we ever keep
            are those we give away.*

*T he only person who likes a smart-ass
            is a donkey trainer.*

Advice is like mushrooms.
　　　　　The wrong kind can kill you.

Thanksgiving was never meant to be
　　　　　confined to a day in November.

D.J.

Kindness is a language which the
　　　　　deaf can hear and the blind can see.

Mark Twain

The one who does not have
　　　　　Christmas in his heart
　　　　　　　　will not find it under the tree.

Quick Quips & Quotes

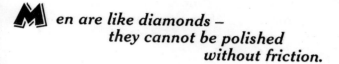

Men are like diamonds –
    they cannot be polished
        without friction.

My sweetest dream is to be
    old and wise.

D.J.

Most of us would get along very well
    if we used the advice
        we give to others.

Faultfinding is like window washing.
    All of the dirt seems to be
        on the other side.

You can do a lot more with a nice word
and a gun than you can
with just a gun!

Al Capone

Do you remember this from school?

"We hold these truths to be self evident,
that all men are created equal; that they are
endowed by their Creator with inherent and
inalienable rights; that among these, are life,
liberty, and the pursuit of happiness; that to
secure these rights, governments are
instituted among men, deriving their just
powers from the consent of the governed;
that whenever any form of government
becomes destructive of these ends, it is the
right of the people to alter or abolish it, and
to institute new government.

Thomas Jefferson wrote that, in the original
Declaration of Independence,

Quick Quips & Quotes

A free people claim their rights
as derived from the laws of nature,
and not as the gift
of their chief magistrate.

Thomas Jefferson.

S ometimes it is said that man cannot be trusted with the government of himself. Can he, then, be trusted with the government of others? Or have we found angels in the form of kings to govern him? Let history answer this question.

Thomas Jefferson in his first inaugural speech in 1801.

D on't climb the corporate ladder.
Take the elevator.

*M*en think computers should be referred
to as females because;

1. No one but the creator understands
their internal logic.

2. The language they use to
communicate with other computers is
incomprehensible to everyone else.

3. The message "Bad command or file
name" is about as informative as
"If you don't know why I'm mad at you,
I'm certainly not going to tell you."

4. Your smallest mistakes are stored in
long-term memory for later retrieval.

5. As soon as you make a commitment to
one you find yourself spending half
your paycheck on accessories for it.

Quick Quips & Quotes

Women think computers should be
referred to as males because;

1. They have a lot of data
but they are still clueless.

2. They are supposed to help you solve
problems, but half of the time
they are the problem.

3. As soon as you commit to one you
realize that if you had waited a
little longer you could have
obtained a better model.

4. In order to get their attention
you have to turn them on.

5. A big power surge will knock them out
for the rest of the night.

J ob Seeker- how much will you pay me?
    Boss – I'll pay you what you're worth!
J ob Seeker – I don't work for
                  anyone that cheap!

T ime cannot be influenced by mankind. It gives each of us a beginning and an end, and this makes us question the significance of what comes between. But... if you can create something time cannot erode, something which ignores the eccentricities of particular eras or moments... Something that is truly timeless, this is the ultimate victory."

Dr. Ing H.C.F. Porch

Quick Quips & Quotes

I 'd love to go but the last time I went
I never came back.

T here is something gratifying in doing
something that does not
have to be the best.

W ork is a wondrous thing.
We say we hate it and
some time seek to avoid it,
but it captures our emotions
and gratifies our pride.

Y ou never think of water
until the well goes dry.

S hut up! If you listen,
          you may learn something.

L ife is a test. It is only a test! Don't worry.
    You'll never get out of it alive anyway.

I f you had only one hour to live and could
    make only one phone call, who would
    you call and what would you say—
    and why are you waiting?

               Stephen Levine.

I f you really don't know whose turn it is to
    throw out the trash,
         throw it out yourself.

Quick Quips & Quotes

*T*hose who go to sea for pleasure
would go to hell for a pastime.

*G*ossips get caught in mouth traps.

*W*hen you're through changing,
you're through.

*W*ise men aren't always silent
but they know when to be.

*H*ousework is something
you do that nobody notices
until you don't do it.

Doing nothing for others is the
undoing of us.

Don't grumble because roses have thorns.
Rejoice that thorns have roses.

Trouble is the structural steel
used in building character.

Too old to set a bad example,
one starts giving good advice.

Alcoholics commit suicide
a little bit at a time.

114

Quick Quips & Quotes

 would rather that people question
    why there wasn't a statue of me in the
town square than to have them
    question why there was one.

Burton Rafael

H *e who has not looked upon sorrow*
    cannot see joy.

"The Eye of the Prophet" by Kahlil Gibran

A *jury consists of 12 people chosen*
    to decide who has a better lawyer.

Robert Frost

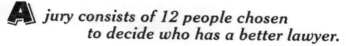 *n order to enjoy the pleasure of your visit,*
    I had to suffer the
    sorrow of your departure.

D.J.

*T*he one word you never want to hear
in the operating room is "oops."

*N*ever wear a backward baseball cap to a
job interview – unless
you're applying for the job of umpire.

*N*ever hit a man with glasses.
Hit 'em with something
bigger and heavier.

*N*ever accept a drink from a urologist.

*N*ever stand between a dog
and a fire hydrant.

Quick Quips & Quotes

A journey of a thousand miles
begins with the first step.

Chinese proverb

T he secret of being tiresome
is to tell everything.

Voltaire

A ll men are innocent until
they run out of money.

E xpert – anyone from out of town.

F riction is a drag.

He who laughs last is probably your boss.

If rabbit's feet are so lucky,
    what happened to the rabbit?

It is better to be wise than to be smart.

It's easier to do good than be good.

Jealousy – all the fun you think they have.

Judge people by what they are;
    not by where they are.

Quick Quips & Quotes

Laughter lubes life's engine.

Lose weight – eat stuff you hate.

Baby sitter – a teenager who is required to
act like an adult while the adults
go out and act like teenagers.

Computer addict – a mouse potato.

What's the difference between
a day off and an off day?

Show me a home with kids and I'll show
you a home where every deck of
cards counts no more than 48.

What lies in our power to do,
lies in our power not to do.

He who conquers others is strong;
he who conquers himself is mighty.

The tragedy of life is not that a man loses
but that he almost wins.

Everybody brings joy to the world;
some by coming and some by leaving.

Quick Quips & Quotes

 minute's success pays the
failure of years.

Robert Browning

ll you need is love.

John Lennon

 What's the difference between lawyers
and computers?

 Computers get twice as intelligent and
half as expensive every two years.

hat is strength without wisdom?

There is no pain in the wound received
in the moment of victory.

*F*armer to female hunter; OK, lady! OK!
It's a deer.
Just let me get my saddle off of it!

*I*ntelligence is like underwear.
We should all have it
but we shouldn't show it off.

*T*hirty days has Septober, April, June and
Nowonder. All the rest have thirty-one
except Grandma
and she smokes a pipe.

*W*omen have PMS. Men have ESPN.

Quick Quips & Quotes

*To know, yet to think that one does not
know is the best. Not to know,
yet to think that one knows,
will put one in difficulty.*

Loa Tzu, Toa Te Ching

Fools despise wisdom and instruction.

Proverbs 1:7

*Knowledge is knowing facts.
Wisdom is knowing how
to use those facts.*

*Life is an uphill bike ride.
You have to keep on pedaling.*

The lust for power is not a sign of strength. Indeed, it is a sign of weakness.

Manners – traffic rules for society.

Somewhere between puberty and adulthood there is a door that opens and lets the future in.

If there was a major internet blackout, nearly one million computer nerds would have to go out and get a life.

Jay Leno

At least the airlines are considerate enough to give you small portions of their food.

Quick Quips & Quotes

I am a cookie connoisseur.
>   My grand daughter is a girl scout.

D.J.

A   I saw you last night
B   I saw you see me
A   I saw you see me see you
B   I saw you see me see you see me

D.J.

Bad planning on your part does not
>   necessarily constitute an
>>   emergency on my part

If you think experience is costly,
>   try ignorance.

For he who seeks truth
and tells it to humanity
must expect to suffer.

Kahlil Gibran

Gee Grandpap, you played baseball
with a wooden bat?

One of the toughest things to imagine is
that you are not smarter than average.

I'm just like a baseball umpire;
when I'm doing things right,
nobody notices me!

To use bad English is regrettable.
To use bad Scotch is unforgivable.

Quick Quips & Quotes

Be kind, for everyone you meet
is fighting a harder battle.

Plato

If you would be loved, love and
be lovable.

Benjamin Franklin

Irish toast: May you be in heaven three
days before the devil
knows you're dead.

I saw man conceal his cowardice
beneath the mantle of patience,
call laziness tolerance,
and fear, courtesy.

Kahlil Gibran

After all, the strongest weapon of all
is a kind and gentle word.

I'd like to help you out.
Which way did you come in?

I went on a diet for 2 weeks. I lost 14 days.

D.J.

The worst thing is to be somebody
to nobody.

Mother Teresa

If you want to lead the orchestra,
you must turn your back to the crowd.

Quick Quips & Quotes

I 'd like to compliment you on your work.
When are you going to start?

S ome people come into our lives
and quickly go. Some stay for a while
and leave footprints on our
hearts and we are never,
ever the same.

W edding cake - a food that greatly
reduces the sex drive.

E njoy yourself. These are the good old
days you're going to miss
in the days ahead.

Smith and Wesson beats 4 aces.

Bumper sticker on red neck's truck.

The task ahead of us is never as great as the power behind us.

Alcoholics Anonymous

Of course you can have it all. You just can't have it all at once.

A pipe gives a wise man time to think and a fool something to stick in his mouth.

Quick Quips & Quotes

And I saw lawmakers in idle discussion,
selling their wares
on the steps of deceit
and hypocrisy.

Kahlil Gibran

The worst prison is a closed heart.

Pope John Paul II

Carrying anger is a heavy load.

The Half Fast Research Company reports
that 9 out of 10.

Chickens and people are alike in that the
more you give them, the less likely
they are to scratch for themselves.

The most predictable thing about the stock
market is the number of experts
who claim to have predicted it.

A $300.00 picture tube will protect
a .10 cent fuse by blowing first.

Nature always sides with the hidden flaw.

Quick Quips & Quotes

We should be careful to get
out of an experience only the
wisdom that is in it.

Mark Twain

A bird in the hand is better
than one overhead.

Everyone has a scheme for
getting rich that will not work.

Intelligence is like a river.
The deeper it is,
the less noise it makes.

With over 6 billion people in the world,
what are the chances
of this being your day?